FISH TAILS

Writers

Emily Thornton Calvo

David Schecter

Paul Seaburn

Lynda Twardowski

new seasons®

As soon as you
discover a good spot,
everybody finds out!

"He ate my pet minnow!"

Waiting to fish with baited breath.

After catching a
tire in the river,
Tom figured he
could catch a
fish in the road.

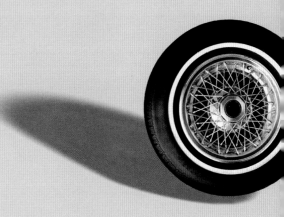

13

Will she ever
compete with
fishing?

Marcia catches two fish and one whale.

Filet of Sole

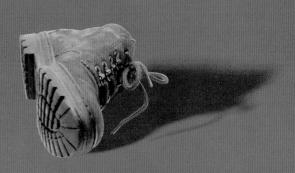

There was no way this crew was ready for one more passenger!

"**H**ey, Dad! If you caught this fish, how come there's a bar code on the side?"

"I gave him a dirty look, and he just jumped out of the water."

"**W**ill Grandma cook 'im, even
if he's just a minnow?"

When they're not biting...

When it comes to fishing, Amy just won't get off Jeff's back.

Apparently Nemo took a wrong turn.

33

Even nerds get lucky once in a while.

Fishing makes your dreams come true.

37

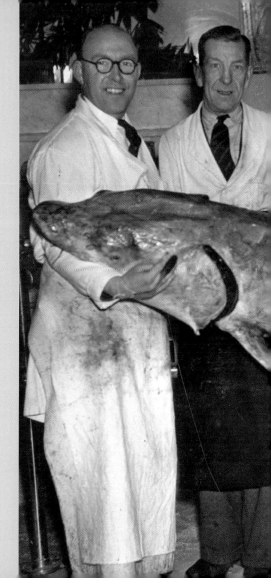

"Now if I can just convince my wife to mount it on the living room wall."

Annette got the catch of the day, but Charlie got the catch of a lifetime.

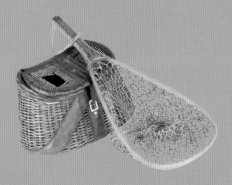

Live in the woods, sleep all winter, and fish every day—it's every angler's dream.

The real reason men fish.

"Who said I need a license to fish?"

"You're scaring away the fish!"

Donald's fish fry menu was looking pretty grim.

They may smell bad now but
wait until we fry them.

"I want a cat—
not a catfish!"

It's great to catch something
besides a cold.

Melvin promised his mother
he would wear a tie every Sunday.

Dad remembered everything for our big fishing trip to Minnesota except for the hotel reservations.

"Gee, no wonder this guy's catchin' nothin'. These worms taste awful."

"Is your brother really paying us ten bucks to catch a fish while he's taking our picture?"

"I'm up to my neck in fishing."

67

Some anglers
elevate fly casting
to an art form.

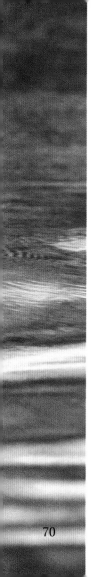

Lenny can concentrate better when his mouth is full.

"Nah Nah . . . try to catch me now!"

What you do when you
run out of bait.

•➤

"**W**hy don't we just
let this one go?"

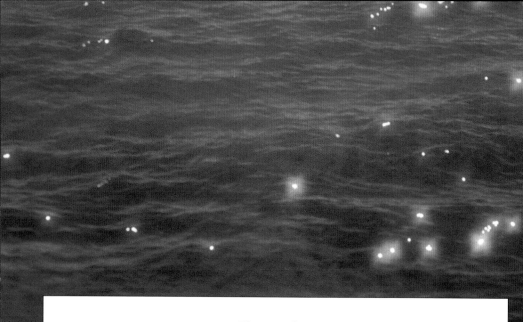